PURSUING
THE Journey of a Worshipper
PRESENCE
OF GOD

Chris and Jennie Orange

ALouderVoice

British Library Cataloguing-in-Publication Data
A catalogue record for this book is available from the British Library

ISBN 978-0-9563902-0-2

Cover and text design: Santamaria Design Consultants
167 Southwood Lane, Highgate, London N6 5TA
mail@santamaria.co.uk

Editorial: Jenny Page

This book is dedicated to
Wes Sutton, father and mentor,
who taught us to love His presence

The wonder of the cross
Our Saviour crucified
His mercy reaching out to us
Redeeming sacrifice
Who can comprehend
The burden that He bore
Carrying our sin and shame
To bring us near to God

Contents

Foreword

by Dr Gregory A. Boyd

Several times over the last eight years I have had the privilege of ministering in services at which Chris and Jennie Orange led worship. In all honesty, I have rarely sensed the presence of God as tangibly and with such power as I have in these services. It's not because these two people are such gifted musicians and singers, though they certainly are that. It's because they *know what worship is all about.*

It's *not* about the music. It's *not* about singing. It's not even primarily about the lyrics. It's about coming into the presence of God. The art of worship-leading is about knowing how to use music, singing and lyrics to help usher others into God's presence. I know of no one who does this better than Chris and Jennie Orange, and I'm absolutely ecstatic that they have now felt led to put their insights into this little book to help other worship leaders.

How desperately the church today needs the biblical, spiritual and practical insights contained in this book! Far too many congregations treat worship like a nice 'sing-along' or, even worse, as a time to enjoy a musical performance. Too many others view worship as something Christians are just 'supposed to do' once a week because this is what the church has always done. Most people in these churches have no idea how much of the vibrant life of God they are missing because of this.

As Chris and Jennie so profoundly understand, worship is the heartbeat of the church! As worship goes, *so the church goes*. Things happen in worship that simply cannot happen anywhere else. True worship leads us into God's presence, and it's here where our head knowledge about God becomes a transforming experience of God. When we come into God's presence through worship, the Spirit can begin removing the cataracts from our spiritual eyes so that we can behold the glory of Jesus Christ more clearly, and be transformed into his image more completely (2 Corinthians 3 vs 17–18). When we come into God's presence through worship, the Spirit can begin to melt the calluses that often form around our hearts so that we can sense God's love more profoundly, experience his peace more sweetly and enjoy his goodness more intensely.

Yet, by God's own design, the quality of a congregation's worship largely hinges on the giftedness and anointing of the worship leader. In this book, leaders will find indispensable biblical insights into the nature of worship, an abundance of spiritual disciplines that must characterise a worship leader and a wealth of experience-filled suggestions on confronting common challenges in worship-leading. Most importantly, if this book is taken to heart and read prayerfully, I believe worship leaders will find their own passion to enter God's presence rekindled. They will be stirred never to settle but instead always to hunger for more of God's presence. Because wherever we and our congregation may be at in terms of the depth and passion of our worship, there always remains more of God to know, experience and love.

My prayer is that God use this labour of love on the part of Chris and Jennie to equip and inspire a multitude of worship leaders to usher people into the tangible, sweet and powerful reality of God's presence.

Dr Gregory A. Boyd
Senior Pastor, Woodland Hills Church, St Paul, Minnesota, USA, author of *The Myth of a Christian Nation*, *Letters from a Skeptic* and *God at War*
gregboyd.org

Foreword
by Faith Forster

Chris and Jennie Orange came to Ichthus in 2002 as part of our mentoring programme, Radical Network. They stayed on to take up the mantle of worship leaders for the Ichthus movement, and have been a blessing and an inspiration to us ever since. In return, they have found fruitfulness in their lives and ministry. They came at a time of turmoil and difficulty for us and for the movement, and it was in part their fervent pressing through in worship, and in releasing streams of God's Spirit and grace, that helped us to keep our own feet steady and our spirits refreshed and renewed in God as we forged the way ahead. We found the truth once again that worshipping our faithful God strengthens at all times, and brings us through the darkest night!

It is a privilege and a responsibility to lead God's people in worship, and Chris and Jennie understand that and live it. In these pages they share profound truths and practical insights that have helped them to keep pressing into God. Their experiences make this an invaluable handbook for every worship leader, but there is also much here to help pressured pastors to understand spiritual dynamics. Here you will find tips to help people focus on the Lord, to find agreements growing in the atmosphere of worship, and the reminder that worship releases spiritual power to overcome the evil one.

It has been said that as God is always at hand, we come to Him by turning, not by travelling. This is profoundly true, but sometimes the turning is only the beginning of a spiritual pilgrimage into the heart of God. This was true for the Prodigal Son in Luke 15, as he turned his heart towards home and began his journey back to His Father. Even then, the Father shortened his journey by running to meet him! This is the experience of everyone who presses into God in worship – we find Father waiting for us, pouring His love on us and opening His own heart to us.

What a privilege to be involved in such an activity, such a ministry! Thank you, Chris and Jennie, for inspiring us in this. May you inspire many others through your lives and words!

Faith Forster
Co-founder of Ichthus
Christian Fellowship
London, UK
ichthus.org.uk

The Journey Begins . . .

Chris

My journey with Jesus began when I was eleven years old. I grew up in a Christian family, and apparently gave my heart to Jesus when I was a small boy, but responded to the gospel again at a tent mission in a local park just before my teenage years began. From that day on I felt a longing for the presence of God, and over the next few years I spent as much time as possible hanging around people who inspired me to pursue the things of God.

After experiencing a strong call to serve the Lord at the age of eleven, I expected to walk straight into ministry when I left school at eighteen. But to my surprise, God had other ideas. There is a big difference between hearing the call to serve and being ready to walk in that calling, and for the next ten years the Lord worked on my heart to form character – which He is still doing – in order to prepare me for service.

I discovered that often God will use the practical experiences of life to shape and form character within us in order that we may grow spiritually. As I worked in various secular jobs, and spent some time in unemployment, He used the frustration and doubt caused by waiting for His promises to be fulfilled to fashion my heart into that of a worshipper. I began to understand that all ministry flows from friendship with God, and that it is truly all about Jesus. He isn't looking for the next superhero to enter the Christian scene and transform the church and the world. He is looking for friends who will count it a great honour to serve at His table, and use whatever gifts He has trusted them with for His service and glory.

The ministry of worship is one of God's greatest gifts to the church, through which we are encouraged, strengthened and empowered as we turn our eyes to Him. As I spent time in worship and seeking His face, I was drawn deeper into His presence, and the longing inside of me to know Him and serve Him grew ever stronger. I heard Bill Johnson from Bethel Church, California once say that God reveals Himself to us in worship gradually so that we continue to be drawn deeper as we see more of His face, and this reflected my own journey of worship during some very frustrating years. Rather like David, I was being kept in the hidden place to learn how to worship – something we'll go on discovering for ever – and how to lay my gift down before Him, so that I might live solely for Jesus and not for my own gain or glory.

Even though I'm still at the beginning of this journey of discovery of true worship, I hope and pray that our book will encourage you to pursue the presence of God with all your heart, carving out a friendship with the friend of sinners – Jesus!

Jennie

I am very grateful to have a rich heritage in music. From my early years I can remember my parents leading worship at conferences, and singing at various weddings and meetings. My grandparents were Salvationists, and were involved in choirs and bands for many years. My grandma played all over the world in the ATS band during the Second World War, and then, in later years, played the piano in the Baptist church. Her father had also been a pianist and choirmaster in the Salvation Army. It is not surprising, then, that my sister, brother and I all took to music in various ways.

When I was child, I developed a love for singing. I loved musicals (and still do!) and singing along to them, and so when the opportunity came to sing a solo at my junior school, I relished it. Through my teenage years, I would sing at school concerts, and get so excited about choosing the next song. My faithful sister would learn the piano accompaniment to whichever ballad I had landed on, and I would have the easier task of belting it out!

Then, as a self-conscious teenager, I began to sing with

my dad as he led worship in our church, and that's when things began to change. I remember the first moment when I felt I'd touched something eternal. It was so different to singing for my own accolade. It fulfilled me – literally, filled me up – with something that was so much better than self. It was Jesus.

Today, there is still nothing quite like it. There is nothing like touching the Eternal One from earth, whether that be as my heart burns within me as I read the Scriptures, or know His voice as I pray, or feel His presence as I sing to Him in worship. It's the place where I know who I am, and begin to grasp more of who He is.

I love opening the way for others to touch the Eternal One too, and that's why I love to lead worship. There is something incredibly humbling as you look out at a congregation who are meeting with Jesus. I am very often reminded of a line from the song 'King of Kings, Majesty' that says, 'In royal robes I don't deserve, I live to serve Your majesty.' That sums things up for me.

My prayer as you read this book is that you know the Eternal One afresh, and that you are filled up and inspired by Him to keep pursuing more of heaven on earth.

Introduction

The call to be a worshipper invites us to partake in an exciting, life-changing journey that will draw us deeper and deeper into the presence of the Lord, with each encounter leaving us hungry for more of Jesus. We are called into His presence with singing and into His courts with praise, and it is through the blood of Jesus (called by the writer of Hebrews 'a new and living way', Hebrews 10 v. 20) that we are able to enter the throne room itself. In that place we discover afresh how to worship. The more of Jesus we see, the more we learn what it means to surrender our lives to Him. As we learn to cultivate a place in our hearts where we can dwell in His presence, the Lord is able to shape and mould us to become like Him.

The task of a worship leader comes with great responsibility and privilege as we discover how to take the journey even further, and lead others into the presence of God with us. This comes with all kinds of blessings and challenges as the enemy actively seeks to pressure those who carry this mantle, but we can take heart because the Lion of the tribe of Judah has conquered, and in Him we can overcome.

This book has been written to help lay some foundations

for your worship ministry. Whether you're just starting out as a worship leader, have served for many years, or are simply a worshipper, we want to be able to explore some of the key aspects involved in going deeper in our personal worship life, as well as offer some guidance on leading others in worship. We will look at how to prepare for a meeting, how to lead people effectively and choose songs, as well as pursuing the manifest presence of God personally and understanding the spiritual dynamics of corporate worship. It is in no way an exhaustive study of worship, but instead we hope to inspire you to seek the presence of God in your life and ministry, and lead your congregations in worship in the best and most effective way possible.

1 Preparing for His Presence: Total Surrender

What does the Bible first teach us about worship?
The first recorded act of worship in the Bible is in Genesis 4, where Cain and Abel bring their offerings to the Lord. Cain, a tiller of the ground, brings 'an offering . . . of the fruit of the ground' and Abel, a keeper of flocks, brings 'the firstlings of his flock and of their fat portions' (Genesis 4 vs 3–4). We are told that the Lord had regard for Abel and his offering – in other words, they were pleasing to Him – but for Cain's He had no regard. The difference between these brothers is that Abel brought the best of the best (according to Matthew Henry, 'not the lame, nor the lean, nor the refuse but the firstlings of his flock – the best he had, and the fat portions – the best of the best'), but Cain did not. Even that which Abel offered, he offered 'by faith' (Hebrews 11 v. 4) knowing that he could not give the Lord what He truly deserved.

In essence, Cain's heart was far off, whereas Abel's heart was totally given over to the Lord. His outward gifts were the expression of his inward attitude. Similarly, what we bring before the Lord reveals the state of our own heart.

In Genesis 22, Abraham obediently prepares to

sacrifice his only son Isaac and, in doing so, teaches us that a *worshipping heart* needs to be a *surrendered heart.* This is the first mention of the word 'worship' in the Bible, and it is not coincidental that it comes in the context of surrender, and more particularly, in relation to an event which so clearly foreshadows the cross, when Jesus will offer Himself up in the greatest act of surrender in history ('yet not as I will, but as You will', Matthew 26 v. 39).

The Old Testament continues with further shadows of the cross, with many detailed accounts of the worship that took place in the temple. Sheep and other animals were sacrificed daily for the sins of Israel, in order that the people could remain in fellowship with their God. These sacrifices demonstrate that worship is costly. Faith Forster says that in order for worship to take place, something has to die. Ultimately, the price for us to worship, for us to remain in fellowship with the Lord, has been paid by Jesus on the cross, but now we must also die to our flesh in order that we may live by the Spirit.

This is the cost of being a worshipper. We die to self and say, 'Not my will but Yours be done.' We are called to echo David's sentiments when he pays Araunah for a field in which he wishes to sacrifice to the Lord, refusing to be given it without payment because of his position. He says, 'I will not offer burnt offerings to the Lord

my God which cost me nothing' (2 Samuel 24 v. 24).
Worship without cost is worthless. We must be those
who surrender to the Lord – our souls, our lives, our all.

*Take a moment now in quiet to lay everything down
again before the Lord: your life, gifting, dreams, work and
family – all that you are – and allow yourself to be totally
surrendered in His arms. Use your imagination to picture
Jesus taking everything, and simply rest in this place of
surrender.*

2 A Heart for His Presence

What can we learn from the life of David?

The first account of David's life in the Bible (1 Samuel 16) provides us with an understanding of the credentials God is looking for in those who will serve Him. Samuel is sent by the Lord to Jesse's house to anoint the next king of Israel. Previously, he has crowned Saul king, and Saul is described in 1 Samuel 9 v. 2 as being taller and more handsome than those around him. Therefore when Samuel stands before the sons of Jesse, he expects their outward qualities to be the deciding factor in choosing a suitable successor. Yet when Samuel stands before Eliab, the eldest son, thinking that he is surely the chosen one, God says to him, 'Do not look at his appearance or at the height of his stature, because I have rejected him; for God sees not as man sees, for man looks at the outward appearance, but the Lord looks at the heart' (1 Samuel 16 v. 7).

Our ability to please the Lord and serve Him effectively has nothing to do with how good we appear on the outside, but on the condition of our hearts. It is not to do with how proficient we are on our instrument, how many prayers we are seen to pray or how 'well' we appear to live our lives to those around us, but rather it is about what is on the inside. Integrity of heart is fundamental if we are to be those who carry the Holy Spirit in our lives, and it is the Holy Spirit in us that will make us effective for Him. David, who became very aware of this, wrote, 'Behold, You desire truth in the innermost being' (Psalm 51 v. 6). As he progressed through life he grew to understand the absolute necessity of a clean heart, and was desperate to regain this condition after he had committed adultery. In Psalm 51 vs 10–11 he cries, 'Create in me a clean heart, O God, and renew a steadfast spirit within me. Do not cast me away from Your presence and do not take Your Holy Spirit from me.' There is a clear link here between the state of our hearts and the presence of His Spirit with us. As we keep our hearts clean, as we live with integrity, the Holy Spirit is welcomed within us and we can be used for His glory.

If we truly want to pursue the presence of the Lord, we have a responsibility to keep our hearts clean. Like David, we need to be those who allow the Lord to mould and shape us through the fire of His presence, in order that we too would be a prophetic voice to our generation, calling them to worship.

David, the worshipper: a worshipping heart
Though no one but a few sheep could see David as he played, sang and meditated, the Lord could see him, and

He used that time to cultivate David's character. As a result of the investment he made in worshipping in the hidden place, David gained authority in the Spirit and was therefore ready to be called and anointed by God.

These days, our culture is so saturated and obsessed with celebrity status that we feel the need to throw ourselves forward in case we're not discovered. While there is nothing new in this (Lucifer turned from giving the glory to God to wanting it for himself), in our society today 'fame' has seemingly become much more possible. The problem with this is that we weren't made to be worshipped, we were made to be worshippers, and if we gladly receive worship from others, it will end up destroying our own worship to the Lord.

Today many of our churches are set up with the musicians in everyone's gaze. It is no longer the pulpit or the altar or the Communion table that is in the centre, but the worship leader and the band. This is not wrong in itself, but if our hearts are not totally surrendered to the Lord, if we are not looking for His glory alone, then it can become a stumbling block. Instead of saying, 'Hallowed be Your name', our prayer can become, 'Hallowed be my name'.

Over the years, we have prayed that we would be invisible, that only Jesus would be remembered as we lead worship. We do not see ourselves as somehow separate from the congregation, but rather as worshippers together with the common purpose of lifting up *His* name, not our own.

There are often two issues in view if a person seems to desire the 'limelight', and these are insecurity and pride. Both of these issues will lead to spiritual death if they are not addressed in prayer. Insecurity will need to feed continually on praise and affirmation, and will seek out relationships that provide this. Insecurity will end up killing the life of the Spirit as it focuses on self and not on Jesus. Herod's insecurity, his fear that someone might take his place, led him to kill all the Hebrew boys from nought to two years (Matthew 2 v. 16). He stopped at nothing to ensure that he still had prime place.

Equally, pride will also kill spiritual life. In Acts 12 vs 21–23 Herod sits in his fine royal apparel on the great rostrum and begins to deliver an address. The people begin to cry out that his voice is the voice of a god and not a man, and because he does not give glory to God, he is struck down and eaten by worms! The result of pride here is death. Let us not be those who touch the glory of God and by doing so cause the life of the Spirit to disappear from our churches. It is all too easy to do, and the devil comes subtly as he did in the Garden of Eden. Our decision, our pursuit, must be to be like Christ, who, although He existed in the form of God, did not regard equality with God a thing to be grasped, but emptied Himself and humbled Himself, taking the form of a bondservant (Philippians 2 vs 6–8). We do not have a God who came to be served but to serve, to wash others' feet, and we must do likewise. Worship-leading is a service, worship leaders and their teams are servants. If we don't want to serve, then we are simply performers, and we will not lead people into the presence of God.

David didn't push himself forward or try to manipulate circumstances to his advantage. He learned to serve as he cared for the sheep on the hillside, and he was known by God. 1 Corinthians 8 v. 3 says, 'If anyone loves God, he is known by Him.' The Father could trust David with a high calling because of the love relationship they had cultivated. His heart was totally surrendered.

David's secret place was not always battle-free. We are told that he would chase after lions and bears, and wrestle and kill them when they came after his sheep, even snatching sheep from their jaws (1 Samuel 17 vs 34–35). Similarly, our secret places are not always battle-free, but they are a training ground for future battles for us, as they were for David. If we can learn to overcome in the secret place, then we will gain authority and experience when we need to overcome our 'goliaths'.

The wellspring that David had dug in worship in the secret place is also in evidence when Saul calls for him to minister on his harp. The Spirit of God had left Saul, and he was being tormented by a demonic spirit. He instructed his servants to find a skilful musician to play before him, to give him refreshment (1 Samuel 16 v. 17). David was selected as he was known for his skill, and as he played the evil spirit would depart from Saul (1 Samuel 16 v. 23). The devil hates to hear the praises of God, and as David worshipped on the harp, as he had done thousands of times when no one was watching, the demonic spirit was forced to leave as the presence of God fell in the throne room of King Saul. Time invested in pursuing the presence of God in the secret place gives us confidence when we need to release His presence upon others.

David, the king: a steadfast heart
David suffered many setbacks in his journey to become king. Having been anointed for the task as a ruddy, handsome youth in 1 Samuel 16, it would seem that the coronation should follow imminently. Yet even after he had defeated Goliath, married the king's daughter and been rewarded with position and honour for his valour, there were still many battles and much heartache to come between his anointing and his coronation aged thirty (2 Samuel 5).

Like David, many of us also face challenges and

opposition to our calling before it is established. Just after Jesus was baptised and about to begin His public ministry, the devil opposed Him and attempted to undermine who He was and derail the mission before it had even begun (Luke 4). What was essential for Jesus as He faced this time of challenge was the presence and the leading of the Holy Spirit. It is also essential for us. Jesus returned from the Jordan *full of the Holy Spirit*, He was *led around* the wilderness *by the Spirit* and He returned to Galilee *in the power of the Spirit*. If we are to be those who hold fast to our calling, then we must live our lives in the presence of the Holy Spirit, following His leading. Jesus returned from the desert having overcome the enemy, and began His public ministry with the confidence that He knew who He was and what He was called for. In the same chapter of Luke, He goes on to declare His manifesto from Isaiah 61.

When we live by the Spirit, we learn how to wait for all that the Lord has for us rather than attempt to make things happen in our own strength. During David's lonely years spent as a fugitive outcast in enemy territory, he was pursued by Saul and attacked in an attempt to destroy the calling on his life. However, David's worshipping heart was steadfast, and He waited for the Lord to establish him as king rather than take the throne by force. A worshipping heart looks to the Giver, not the gift. Worship will keep you looking towards Jesus Himself, rather than to the ministry He gives. When we learn this, we can be trusted with much. Even when he was presented with the opportunity to murder King Saul in 1 Samuel 24 vs 3–7, he would not touch the Lord's anointed but rather left it in God's hands to make a way for him. David demonstrates incredible respect for the anointing by sparing Saul's life, and therefore is entrusted with a vast kingdom when he finally becomes king. If we can learn to respect the anointing as David did, the Lord will be able to trust us with more and more of His Spirit for His work.

David, the warrior: a courageous heart

Having been anointed by the prophet Samuel and called by King Saul to minister in his courts, David then shows his courageous nature as he contends with Goliath. Hearing Goliath's challenge to the Israelites, David offers himself to Saul to fight the Philistine, but the King attempts to dissuade him, saying, 'You are not able to go against this Philistine to fight with him; for you are but a youth while he has been a warrior from his youth' (1 Samuel 17 v. 33). However, David assuredly asserts, 'The Lord who delivered me from the paw of the lion and from the paw of the bear, He will deliver me from the hand of this Philistine' (1 Samuel 17 v. 37).

Investing time in worshipping our God will deepen our relationship with Him. In short, we will know Him better! The more we know Him, the more confidence we will have in all that He is able to perform. This, then, gives us confidence to face the enemy before us, no matter how large he appears to be, because we have been spending time with the One who is the greatest of all. David destroys Goliath in public having killed lions and bears in private, knowing that it is the same God who fights for Him. Our worship in the secret place will similarly equip us for battle, and will enable us to declare with David: 'I come to you in the name of the Lord of hosts' (1 Samuel 17 v. 45) because we know who this 'Lord of hosts' is, and that He is worthy of our confidence.

David saw many victories as he learned to trust God in all circumstances. In Psalm 56 v. 9–11 he wrote, 'Then my enemies will turn back in the day when I call; this I know, that God is for me. In God, whose word I praise, in the Lord, whose word I praise, in God I have put my trust, I shall not be afraid.'

Let us be those who know the Lord, who know that He is for us, so that we can see our enemies turn back!

3 Gifts for His Presence

It is so important to hold the gift of music lightly in our hands. This precious gift is given to us by the Lord to release His presence, and therefore we must learn how to tame our hearts and use what the Lord has given us skilfully, but with humility. The musical gift should sit on the firm foundation of a life built on Jesus, as this will keep it in submission to the Holy Spirit so that He may use it for His purposes and glory. When we allow ourselves to be seduced by our own gifting, we become vulnerable to pride. This was the route to the fall of Satan, so we must ensure that our hearts are pure and our gifts laid down before we even strike a note in worship.

There is something beautiful about listening to a skilful musician use their gifting to glorify God. It just makes sense! Whereas the reverse is an ugly display that seeks to turn the attention of the listener to the player rather than to the One who created music. Psalm 19 v. 1 says, 'The heavens are telling of the glory of God; and their expanse is declaring the work of His hands.' If you imagine the universe, in all its colour and diversity, in place simply to demonstrate the glory and majesty of our God, it must look ridiculous to heaven when we seek to glorify ourselves through the sounds that He has given us in the first place! The heavens don't declare their own glory but the glory of God, and this is what we have been made to do.

In 2 Samuel 6 David sees first-hand the danger of touching the glory of the Lord. While being carried on a new cart (and not as Moses had prescribed in Exodus 25 vs 14–15 and Numbers 4 v. 15), the ark appears as if it is about to fall, and Uzzah reaches out and takes hold of it. He is struck down by the Lord for his irreverence and dies. It is a stark lesson for David and for those with him, and when he later brings the ark to Jerusalem, he does so with sacrifices, in total reverence. There were specific instructions as to how the ark should be carried because it was a symbol of the presence of God on earth. We should treat the presence of God with no less reverence, and we should certainly never touch His glory. It is all too easy to do but it is empty, futile and offensive to God, and such fleshly attitudes must die if we are to be those who carry His presence. Being involved in worship is not an opportunity to display our gifting before others, but to display Jesus.

Jesus said, 'Where your treasure is, there your heart will be also' (Matthew 6 v. 21). We need to be those whose treasure is Jesus, and Jesus alone. When we take our eyes off Him, they are inevitably drawn to other things. We can become worshippers of music or, even worse, worshippers of self, which before heaven must sound like a 'noisy gong' or a 'clanging cymbal' (1 Corinthians 13 v. 1). However, if we keep the musical gifting in check and seek to be hidden in Him, Jesus will be the sound that people hear as we play and sing.

With our gifting placed in the hands of the Father, we make ourselves available to Him for His purposes. God wants us to be the best we can possibly be, but He is more concerned about the state of our hearts than our talent for playing an instrument. Like the raw materials that are used to create musical instruments, He wants to shape the raw material of our hearts so that they become a clear channel for Him, without any obstacles of pride and self-aggrandisement in the way. Through this clear channel, He is then able to breathe on the sounds we make and create supernatural environments where His will can be done.

Our desire is to see so much more of His will being done as we worship: more healings, more salvation and more freedom for the oppressed. We believe that if musicians and singers will surrender their gifting to God, there will be a new anointing upon worship music that will break the heavy yoke of the enemy and release the captives. Psalm 29 v. 4 tells us that the voice of the Lord is powerful and majestic, and it is *His* voice that we want people to hear. Verse 11 of the same Psalm then tells us that He will give strength to His people and bless them with peace. The powerful and majestic God longs to release His voice through our playing and singing, to bring strength and peace to His people.

Let us, like the psalmist, ask the Lord to search us and know us, to test us and see if there is any offensive way in us (Psalm 139 vs 23–24), so that we might truly surrender our gifts to Him and let *Him* show us how to play!

4 Pursuing His Presence

In every worship session we are ultimately looking for one thing – to break through into the presence of God. The singing and playing are simply vehicles to lead us into the holy place where we can experience Him for ourselves. Our worship is a response to a God who woos us into His presence, where we may enjoy the love He graciously wants to pour into our hearts. In Psalm 27 v. 8 the psalmist writes, 'When You said "Seek My face," my heart said to You, "Your face O Lord, I shall seek." Do not hide Your face from me.' David's desire to seek after God comes as a result of hearing the call of the Lord, who asks us all to seek Him.

Our God is a relational God, and this is reflected not only first and foremost in the Trinity but also in all God's dealings with humankind, from creation to redemption and beyond! It makes sense, then, that we are on a path of discovery to know Him, to mine the depths of His unending love towards us. Our response should be like that of the beloved in Song of Solomon 3 v. 2, who says, 'I must seek him whom my soul loves.' There is a longing and an intensity of feeling here that should be reflected in our attitude when we come to worship. Our life's quest should be to dwell in the presence of God, for He only is the source of true satisfaction. One of the great deceptions in the church is the thought that we have learned 'how' to worship, and therefore don't need to spend much time engaged in it any more. We know how to sing the songs, raise our hands and do all the outward things, but we have only just begun to understand the significance of what we will spend eternity doing – worshipping God.

We need to learn how to soak in His presence and allow our *inner beings* to be *strengthened by His Spirit* (Ephesians 3 v. 16). The more time we give to waiting on Him and receiving His Spirit with grateful hearts, the more we'll discover the power of His love towards us, leaving us captivated as we gaze into the face of Jesus. Some people find it easy to worship for long periods of time, whereas others find it more difficult to sustain, but we all need to be stretched. With this in mind, as those involved in worship we must help people to remain longer and bring 'a sacrifice of praise'. This principle is similar to the 'pain barrier' in running. Joggers will speak of a pain that feels like a brick wall against them as they run, but only by keeping going can they reach a new level of strength and energy for the next stage of the race. It is no different when we seek after the presence of God. The pursuit of Him beyond our natural ability will always bring us to a place of greater breakthrough.

This individual commitment to the presence of the Lord will open the way for a corporate manifestation of His presence. Peter describes us as 'living stones' being built into a spiritual house, with Jesus as the cornerstone (1 Peter 2 vs 4–8). Together, we make up a house that God can fill and indwell by His Spirit. In order for us to be a 'sound' building, each 'stone' must take responsibility for its own relationship with God, its own pursuit of Him. Personal commitment to the presence of God will increase the anointing on the church and, as a result, more spiritual life will flow. A people gathered together, having already learned to *press in* individually, will see more supernatural power released corporately, changing the spiritual atmosphere around them.

All music creates an atmosphere, sometimes good, sometimes not so good! At best, it will send you on a journey where you will escape the mundane. At worst, you'll just want to escape! Our worship creates a 'spiritual' atmosphere. As we press into the presence of the Lord, He inhabits our praises and an 'open heaven' is created where healings, provision, peace, salvation and renewed vision of Him are made manifest. Jacob glimpsed this open heaven in Genesis 28. In a dream he saw a ladder with angels ascending and descending from earth to heaven and, when he awoke, he declared, 'How awesome is this place! This is none other than the house of God, and this is the gate of heaven' (Genesis 28 v. 17). Jacob realised that he was under an open heaven, a place where heaven becomes a reality on earth and supernatural activity becomes a normal occurrence.

In John 1 v. 51, Jesus tells Nathanael that he 'will see the heavens opened and the angels of God ascending and descending on the Son of Man'. In other words, where Jesus is, you will also find a release of heaven. Jesus spoke about the Kingdom of Heaven being 'at hand' when He was on the earth, and it kept breaking out as He ministered. As we worship Jesus and pursue His presence, we can expect to experience an open heaven wherever we are, and see our 'atmospheres' and surroundings change. It is a foretaste of Revelation 21 v. 3 when our soon-coming King will dwell with us again: 'Behold, the tabernacle of God is among men, and He will dwell among them, and they shall be His people, and God Himself will be among them, and He will wipe away every tear from their eyes; and there will no longer be any death; there will no longer be any mourning, or crying, or pain; the first things have passed away.'

Chris

In 1998 I received a vision from the Lord that powerfully

impacted my life, and made me begin to pursue the Lord for greater measures of His Spirit in worship. Here is the prophetic vision.

I saw an outdoor stage with a worship band playing and singing. Many people were watching and were being ministered to by the music, and many others continued to arrive until the number was so huge that I began to wonder if the anointing would be enough to cover all the people. But the more people arrived, the more the anointing of His presence increased, and the 'cloud' of His presence covered all who were there. Then I saw Jesus on the cross above the crowd of people. His blood was dripping down onto them, and as this happened God began to minister healing in great power. The healings were so incredible and in such great number that ambulances from local hospitals began to arrive with the sick, and as they got out of the vehicles they were healed. It felt as though the place was an open heaven as the band worshipped Jesus. I felt the Lord speak to me, saying, 'Whatever you can dream, I can do far more. It doesn't matter how way out you think it is, I can do so much more.'

This vision continues to inspire us to press on to new levels of breakthrough into the presence of Jesus because we know that He has the power to change lives, and we want to see heaven here on earth.

There are many inspiring stories of others who have dedicated their lives to seek after 'Him whom my soul loves' (Song of Solomon 3 v. 2). Smith Wigglesworth, an evangelist with an extraordinary healing ministry in the early 1900s, would spend hours in the presence of the Lord, and from this place see incredible healing miracles as he prayed for the sick. When we train our spirits to be constantly awake to the Holy Spirit, we enter a new realm where God is able to release His tangible presence at any time over our lives. We become sensitive to His Spirit, so that we can respond to Him as He asks us to partner with Him in releasing the Kingdom of Jesus.

There is an account in which Smith Wigglesworth was walking down a busy street towards a house where a sick person lay. As he walked, the glory of the Lord fell on him and he stood in the street with tears flowing down his face. So powerfully was the Holy Spirit upon him that he was afraid to speak to anyone in case the presence of the Lord left him. He continued to the house in silence, not engaging in conversation with the girl who was with him. When he arrived at the sick woman's house, he laid his hands on her, and the glory of the Lord filled the house so powerfully that he rushed out into the street. The girl chased after him asking where he got this kind of glory, and Wigglesworth simply answered, 'Go back inside and seek the Lord.' The woman was completely healed of her sickness.

Today, the same manifest presence of the Lord is available to each one of us if we can discipline ourselves to seek Him. There are all kinds of ways to pursue God, and each person needs to find their own way of entering His presence. Personally we have found that it is helpful to use different approaches to keep things fresh and to stretch ourselves. Sometimes we will put on a worship CD and join in with singing, dancing, kneeling and raising our hands. Other times, we may go for a walk and sing in tongues until we feel that we've broken through into His presence. Or we may use silence, and soak up the Word of God as we meditate on various Scriptures, or simply sit in His presence and receive His love. It is beneficial not to always require the use of a worship CD to enter His throne room. God has given each of us the capacity to worship Him, and if we're going to lead others in worship, we need to be able to cultivate a place where we can find Him simply by exercising our spirits without the help of music.

In James, we are promised that if we draw near to God, He will draw near to us (James 4 v. 8). Often our lifestyles and commitments seem to prevent us from 'drawing near', but there is always grace from heaven if we ask for it. Our lives will change, and there will be seasons when we have more time and seasons in which time seems to evaporate altogether, but there is always a way. It will often be the way of sacrifice – less sleep, less entertainment – but it will be worth it.

King David was a man who knew how to pursue God, and when he became king he brought the ark of the Lord to Jerusalem with great dancing and celebration (2 Samuel 6 vs 12–23). 1 Chronicles 23 v. 5 shows us David's passion for worship. We are told that he set apart 4,000 Levites to praise the Lord with instruments he had made, as well as Aaron's sons, 'to sanctify Him as most holy . . . to minister to Him and to bless in His name for ever' (1 Chronicles 23 v. 13). He had a deep commitment to worship, and understood the power that flows from it. Many of his Psalms express his longing for God as he confesses the Lord to be his only hope and source of strength in the face of his enemy. Psalm 26 v. 8 says, 'O Lord, I love the habitation of Your house, and the place where Your glory dwells.' In the very next Psalm, David declares, '. . . in the day of trouble He will conceal me in His tabernacle; in the secret place of His tent He will hide me' (Psalm 27 v. 5). As we enter into the presence of God, His wings cover us and we are safe and can listen to His voice. Knowing that we are in a safe place will help us to open our hearts to receive His word into our lives.

We find examples of people listening to God in the presence of His glory in various places in Scripture.

Ezekiel, having seen a vision of the glory of the Lord, says, 'Such was the appearance of the likeness of the glory of the Lord. And when I saw it, I fell on my face and heard a voice speaking' (Ezekiel 1 v. 28). The glory of the Lord will bring us to our knees, and in this position of humility we will hear His voice. Isaiah has a similar experience. He sees the train of His robe filling the temple in Isaiah 6 v. 1, and then in v. 8 he hears the Lord speaking. Ezekiel and Isaiah, having seen and heard in an atmosphere of worship, took the word of the Lord out to their nation. In our worship times, when we know the Lord is present, we must provide people with the opportunity to listen to His voice. Too often we spend the whole time singing to Him, without allowing any time for Jesus to speak back to us. Worship is born out of relationship, and the interaction between God and His people involves two-way communication.

To be a pursuer of God is an exciting adventure that will transform not only our own lives but also our worship ministries. It is the engine room that fuels our passion for Jesus. Seeking after Him personally will help us become reliant on the Holy Spirit in our everyday lives, and this in turn will give us an ability to minister Him to others. We desperately need a fresh release of the Holy Spirit in the church today, and by becoming those who pursue Him with great passion in our hearts, even through disappointments, we'll lead others to a new and fresh experience of God wherever we are.

Below is a song we wrote which expresses our need for the Holy Spirit today:

Lord let Your presence come
Let glory fill Your house
Christ the eternal King
Come minister in power
We open up our hearts
For You are with us now

Come Holy Spirit
Come Holy Spirit
Be the fire that burns within
To make us holy
Set our hearts ablaze for Jesus
As we wait on You

Christ is the cornerstone
Precious Lamb of God
He made us living stones
A house where glory dwells
We offer up our lives
A living sacrifice

Hope does not disappoint
For love has been poured out
Through the eternal King
His Spirit given now
We lift our hands in faith
Come fill us with Your power

Take time to begin to pursue God in a new and fresh way. Decide now that you'll find a new way to discover His presence with renewed passion. A helpful exercise is to read a small portion of Scripture, and then to spend five or ten minutes praying/singing in tongues to open your heart to the Holy Spirit. When you begin to break through and feel a freedom in your spirit, sit down and wait on Him until you're aware of the presence of Jesus around you. Sometimes it will feel like waves washing over you, and other times you'll simply know He's there in the room. The longer you wait on Him, the more you'll learn to 'tune in' with your spirit and mind. If your thoughts begin to wander onto other things, use your imagination to help you enter His presence. Picture the Lord standing before you, inviting you to 'Come', and gradually your mind will be renewed and come into good spiritual order, and you will find it easier to enter the presence of God.

5 Together for His Presence: Team Dynamics

When we seek spiritual breakthrough, we will often experience a reaction from the enemy. This can manifest itself in various ways, but one of his most ugly schemes is to bring disagreements within our teams, and thereby erode the unity that is so crucial when we are seeking to release the Holy Spirit. It is so important to guard this unity within our teams, as the devil recognises the power that is released when we dwell together in unity. It is our unity within the band that will determine how effectively we release the Holy Spirit: where there is agreement together, the Lord commands the blessing (Psalm 133).

The key to healthy relationships in the band is *prayer*. As a worship leader, and as musicians and singers, it is essential to pray *for* and *with* one another. Prayer develops spiritual relationships. It shapes the way we see each other, and gives us hearts to bless and encourage, rather than to tear down. In the week before you come to lead or to play or sing in worship, spend some time lifting each member of the band to the Lord. During this time, the Lord may highlight individual situations or make you aware of particular schemes of the enemy that you can then pray into. This means you arrive prepared in your heart for all that the Lord wants to accomplish.

Sometimes musical taste can become a source of division in worship teams. Each worship band will have within it a variety of opinions concerning musical style, and this can lead to disagreements over song choices or musical arrangements. It is useful to be aware that the range of opinions within the team may well reflect the opinions of the congregation, too, so it is helpful to take on board what each team member is saying. What is not helpful is a dismissive attitude that says, 'I'm right and you're wrong', as this arrogance is so far removed from the Jesus who laid down His life for the church. If our attitude is one of laying ourselves down for one another, laying down our 'way of doing things' and our particular likes and dislikes, then we will find that the Holy Spirit will aid us, and each person will feel able to be themselves without fear of criticism or ridicule.

One of the most vulnerable times for relationships within the team is during the rehearsal or sound check before a meeting. Time pressures alone can lead to friction within the band and/or PA team, and this is where the prayer that you have invested in the previous week will be so valuable. There are two things that are helpful to remember to overcome difficulties and make the rehearsal a positive experience. First, each team member needs to know that their relationships are more important than their opinions. (Remember the old motto, 'Win the person, not the argument'.) It is better to leave at the end of the meeting knowing that you served the others in the team by sacrificing your idea or musical opinion, rather than getting your own way regardless of who you trampled underfoot.

Second, appoint a musical director within the band. This should be someone who understands the musical dynamics that will shape the songs, and can help steer decisions with grace and humility. The musical director doesn't have to make every decision but will work with the worship leader (if the MD isn't the worship leader) to create arrangements that help them lead confidently. This doesn't put the MD in charge of the worship time, or give them the authority to choose the songs, as the worship leader has the final say over a decision. But it does provide an ordered environment where opinions can be shared and decisions made, without the loudest person always getting their own way!

Let's remember that we are in the worship team to serve each other, the church and, most importantly, the Lord Jesus Christ.

Spend a few moments now praying for your worship team. Picture them in your mind and ask the Lord to bless them and show them His favour. Pray that they may find it easy to enter His presence personally and release His anointing when they worship.

6 Ministering His Presence: Spiritual Dynamics in Worship

We have found that there are a variety of spiritual dynamics to consider when leading worship. When we lift up the name of Jesus, we create an atmosphere where His presence can bring transformation to people's lives. It is our responsibility to know how to lead the church through these different spiritual dynamics, as they will affect the direction of the meeting and help to increase the presence of God.

We are going to highlight seven different spiritual dynamics that help us in our journey into breakthrough. These are the dynamics of *love and adoration*, *celebration and praise*, *intercession*, *theology*, *justice and the poor*, *the prophetic* and *lament*.

Love and adoration
God is love. 1 John 4 vs 15–16 tell us that 'whoever confesses that Jesus is the Son of God, God abides in him, and he in God. We have come to know and have believed the love which God has for us. God is love, and the one who abides in love abides in God, and God abides in him.'

To confess that Jesus is the Son of God is an act of worship, which leads us to intimacy with Him. He relates to us through love, demonstrated at the cross where our journey into His presence always begins (Hebrews 10 v. 19), and where we discover and rediscover the love of Jesus. Nothing can separate us from the love of God (Romans 8 v. 35), the fruit of His Spirit is love (Galatians 5 v. 22). God has proved His love (Romans 5 v. 8), and through His love we are chosen (Ephesians 1 v. 4). These examples give us an understanding of His character, and as we meditate on them in worship, our heart's response is to love Him back.

We only love because He first loved us (1 John 4 v. 19) and gave Himself up for us (Ephesians 5 v. 2). We enter into a relationship that He has forged, fought and won for us. As our hearts grasp the reality of this salvation, we stand in awe and our hearts cannot help but express love and gratitude back to Him. This was exactly the same for the psalmist. If you look through the Psalms, you will find that when the writer expresses his love towards the Lord, it is usually in the context of salvation and deliverance. In Psalm 18 vs 1–3 David sings, '"I love You, O Lord, my strength." The Lord is my rock and my fortress and my deliverer, my God, my rock, in whom I take refuge; my shield and the horn of my salvation, my stronghold. I call upon the Lord, who is worthy to be praised, and I am saved from my enemies.'

We love Him because He first loved us and saved us.

🖐 *Practical tips for worship leaders* Learn to draw your congregation into the arms of a loving Father. This is a necessity, not overindulgence. The vision of His love will always provide refreshment, grace and strength, and will enable people to be healed from brokenness and press on in their journey with God. It is so important to *teach people to abide* in the love of God during our sung worship times, as too often we rush away when the Father has so much to say to His people. We need to *learn how to linger* and receive the love of God. When a couple want to spend quality time together, they don't tend to grab a bite to eat from the nearest fast-food outlet, but rather they go to a restaurant and spend time talking together, 'beholding' one another. We need to have this same attitude when we come to the Lord. David writes in Psalm 27 of *dwelling* in the house of the Lord, *beholding* His beauty and *meditating* in His temple. Let us not rush away.

Let us also not get in the way! It is such a shame when the worship leader ends up being like a waiter who keeps coming to the table at inappropriate moments, disturbing the lovers from their intimate conversation with each other. Keep listening to the Holy Spirit, and let Him guide you as to when to speak, when to sing and when simply to step back and allow the music to facilitate the love encounter.

We need to know how to *let Jesus minister to us* – how to be served by Him, as the disciples were when He washed their feet – so that we can also serve the world in this same spirit of love. Don't be too quick to move people on to faster songs when you're aware that God is pouring out His love over the church. One way of keeping people in this place of intimacy is to *use short songs* or *simple refrains*, which people can sing easily without having to concentrate on looking at the words. Let us be those who, like David, set their heart on beholding the Lord.

'One thing I have asked from the Lord, that I shall seek: that I may dwell in the house of the Lord all the days of my life, to behold the beauty of the Lord and to meditate in His temple' (Psalm 27 v. 4).

Celebration and praise

Psalm 149 v. 6 declares, 'Let the high praises of God be in their mouth, and a two-edged sword in their hand.' Roger Forster, in his book *Prayer*, explains that 'high praise means that heaven is singing and praising along with the people of God, and that, in turn, releases the supernatural activity of God into the earth'. A great calling of the church is to worship with these high praises that cut through the heavenly realms, breaking the negative, demonic spirits around us by releasing the victorious, supernatural presence of Jesus.

There is something very powerful about the church's celebration of the victory of Jesus, which always puts the enemy to flight. It connects us with heaven, and new faith is released, dispelling the lies, depression and unbelief that so often hinder people from finding breakthrough in worship. Such faith enables people to take hold of the promises of God and walk in freedom. We see this in the New Testament when Paul and Silas are literally freed from prison as they praise (Acts 16 vs 25–34). The story gives us a wonderful window into what happens when we truly celebrate and praise God in all circumstances.

Praise releases breakthrough

As Paul and Silas were singing their songs to God, their praises shook the very foundations of the prison house and the doors and chains were unfastened (Acts 16 vs 25–26). This reminds us of Joshua 6, when the Israelites surrounded Jericho and released a shout with the trumpet blast and saw the walls of the city come crashing down. Paul and Silas sang their praise, and the Israelites shouted theirs. There is a place for shouting in worship. In Psalm 27 v. 6 David speaks of offering *sacrifices with shouts* to God, and in Zephaniah 3 v. 17 we read of the Lord rejoicing over us with shouts of joy. The physical act of lifting our voices rouses our spirits, too, and allows us to push past our earthly inhibitions to connect with heaven. We often say that if you lead out with your voice, your spirit will inevitably follow! The psalmist believed this too as he asked, 'Why are you in despair, O my soul? And why have you become disturbed within me? Hope in God, for I shall again praise Him for the help of His presence' (Psalm 42 v. 5). With his mouth he commanded his soul to look towards the Lord. Shouting, and singing too, of the truths of who Jesus is in all circumstances will always lift our spirits towards Him, and take us to a new place of freedom.

Praise releases prisoners
Acts 16 v. 26 tells us that the 'doors were opened and everyone's chains were unfastened'. Faith-filled worship not only released Paul and Silas's chains but also the chains of the other prisoners as well. There is a link between our praise and another person's freedom. As we discover the power of praise, we will see the effect it has on those around us. This puts a responsibility on us to celebrate actively the victory of Jesus, as it not only pleases God but brings others into the freedom of it too.

Praise releases salvation

As Paul and Silas sang their praises to God, the other prisoners listened. Did their hearts long to know what kind of God could make beaten prisoners sing? Did they decide to give their hearts over to Him? Unfortunately, we aren't told how they responded to the message of the gospel, but we have often found that worship can soften the hearts of unbelievers so they can receive Jesus. We have experienced this many times.

On one occasion we were invited to lead a youth worship evening in a community hall. None of the young people knew Jesus, and they'd never heard worship music before. For the larger part of the evening, we praised 'over' the young people while they stood and watched. Then we shared the gospel message with them, and saw about twenty of them wonderfully give their lives to Jesus. The Holy Spirit had used the worship to create a healthy spiritual atmosphere and prepare the hearts of the young people, so that when they heard the truth about Jesus, they were ready to respond to His invitation.

It is our heart's desire to see more and more salvation as we lift up the name of Jesus in worship. We can be assured that the Lord will use every opportunity to touch hearts and communicate with people, whether at a wedding, a celebration or an open-air.

We began this section by quoting Psalm 149 v. 6, 'Let the high praises of God be in their mouth, and a two-edged sword in their hand.' High praises and a sword go hand in hand, as celebration and praise will often lead us into declaration and warfare against the enemy. In his book *Prayer*, Roger Forster writes, 'High praises are intimately linked to warfare. Worship is not only giving love to God – high praises can begin to put the enemy to flight.' He goes on to explain how the church is called to instruct the rulers and authorities in the heavenly places (Ephesians 3 v. 10), and this we do as we worship with high praises. In our rejoicing in the triumph of the cross, we take new ground in the spirit so that God can establish His Kingdom through our worship.

Practical tips for worship leaders Be aware when you're leading worship that the very act of celebration and praise changes the spiritual atmosphere over a place, preparing the ground for salvation and deliverance. It will help to have plenty of 'high praise' songs in our worship sessions, as seeing the greatness of our God lifts the congregation and encourages them to stand in His authority. Celebration and praise are particularly powerful in open-air meetings, as you can proclaim the Kingdom of Jesus over the surrounding community and release His power over the area. We have found that praising Jesus outdoors has helped to prepare the hearts of the people to hear the gospel.

If you struggle to get your congregation to worship, it can be helpful to ask your passionate worshippers to stand in key areas of the church to 'praise' over the congregation. We have found this to be a successful way of bringing life to areas of the church where people haven't previously engaged in worship. In the past, we have sent individual members of the worship team and other worshippers to stand in areas where people didn't sing. Our worshippers would simply lift their hands and praise. What we discovered was that worshipping Jesus is infectious and that, after a while, people would join them and begin to sing and engage with the Lord.

Intercession

We have found our most effective prayer times to come from effective worship sessions. The faith that grows as we worship, as people take hold of the truth of who the Lord is as they sing, is a catalyst to powerful prayer and intercession. We were once leading a four-hour worship session for a congregation, and were waiting on the Lord and singing in tongues, when a man who doesn't play an instrument took hold of a djembe drum and started to hit it as though he were pounding the ground over and over again. For some reason, this act released a desire in the people to begin to cry out to God for the local area. Very quickly, everyone was facing outwards with their hands raised, praying for salvation in the town. No one asked people to pray specifically for this, but the Holy Spirit was leading as the drum was played, and intercession began to rise up.

Worship softens our hearts and focuses our spirits so that we can hear what the Holy Spirit is saying and follow His lead, partnering with what heaven is seeking to do. It aligns us again with *God's* thoughts and *God's* desires, and this agreement is not only effective but also essential if we are to see the Kingdom of Heaven released.

Moses shows us the relationship between worship and intercession. In Exodus 32, having received the tablets containing the Ten Commandments, he returns to find the people of Israel worshipping a golden calf. The Lord, in His anger, tells Moses to take the people and depart to the Promised Land, which He will clear for them with His angel, yet He will not go with them. The angel would drive out the nations and make them victorious, giving the appearance that the Lord was with them, but it would not be so. In effect, Moses is offered the *victory* without the *presence* of the Lord. For a 'presence-pursuer' such as Moses, this seeming triumph is worthless.

It is a challenge for us today as worship leaders to be people whose desire is only for the presence of the Lord and not for the semblance of it. We need to be careful that our worship doesn't 'look like the real thing' without actually containing the presence of Jesus. Integrity in worship flows out of a decision never to step out of His presence.

Under pressure, in this time of difficulty, Moses enters into the presence of the Lord and, by so doing, leads others in worship. We are told that the pillar of cloud would descend and stand at the entrance of the tent, and that all the people would arise and worship (Exodus 33 vs 9–10). As Moses enters at this time, when the people have sinned and removed themselves from the presence of the Lord, he leads the eyes of the Israelites away from their idol and back onto their God.

This is what we do when we stand before the church and lead worship. As we enter His presence, we draw the people away from all the distractions of the world and set their eyes upon Jesus, where they are able to see His face and hear His voice.

Out of this place of intimacy, Moses discovers the mind of God and begins to intercede for Israel. When we enter into His presence, we too will discover the mind of God, and learn to intercede with Him over our own situations. Too often our prayers are aimless and without power, but when we're in the presence of the King we have boldness to ask for His favour. The Lord hears Moses' prayer and changes His mind, and says, 'My presence shall go with you, and I will give you rest' (Exodus 33 v. 14). There is a rest that we gain in worship which fuels us for more prayer, and Moses continues to seek God for a glimpse of His glory.

There is a continual cycle of Moses worshipping and interceding with the Lord, which again brings us back to a relational understanding of God and of worship. In Exodus 34 vs 6–7, God reveals Himself to Moses as he hides in a rock face and, in response, he 'made haste to bow low toward the earth and worship' (Exodus 34 v. 8). Having worshipped, the words that immediately follow are again words of intercession: 'If now I have found favour in Your sight, O Lord, I pray, let the Lord go along in our midst, even though the people are so obstinate, and pardon our iniquity and our sin, and take us as Your own possession' (Exodus 34 v. 9). Let us make it our pursuit not only to love, celebrate and praise in our worship, but also to intercede as we spend time in His presence.

✋*Practical tips for worship leaders* When you're looking to lead the church into a time of intercession through worship, use songs that build faith so that there is already a sense of spiritual breakthrough when people begin to pray. It is so important that we build corporate agreements in the congregation through praise, as these agreements release power. In many ways, singing songs to God is like singing prayers, and it can be effective to get people to sing a line of a song as a prayer for a situation and then continue in the time of worship. By doing this, the atmosphere doesn't have to change as you stop to explain that you're going to pray or intercede, but the prayers are released through the song.

Another way of leading in prayer is to get the congregation to sing in the Spirit over a town or city. This will help to form agreements for breakthrough, and will release prophetic words that can then be prayed into.

Theology

The word of God is 'living and active and sharper than any two-edged sword' (Hebrews 4 v. 12), therefore when we sing the word of God there is power to build up, encourage, challenge and teach the church. The Moravian church had a different choir for every walk of life: a choir for the married, the widowers, the widows, single brethren, single sisters, youth, great girls, little boys, little girls and infants in arms! All of these people could learn the Scriptures as they sang. On Monday morning, when life isn't looking quite as good as it did on Friday evening, people need something to hold on to as they face a new week of challenges. It can be easier for people to remember a melody rather than a sermon, and so the words of our songs have incredible significance in the role of teaching and encouraging the body of Christ.

🖐*Practical tips for worship leaders* Make sure you use a variety of songs and hymns that tell the whole story of Jesus, as well as express our gratitude and love towards Him. A good challenge we were given was to imagine someone visiting our church for one month, hearing only the worship, and then to ask ourselves how much they would learn about Jesus. Would they hear the whole gospel? Would they know of His unconditional love? Would they understand that He is our Healer, our Saviour and our Provider?

The words we sing will make a real impact on people's lives, especially as they hold on to God under pressure, so let's ensure we sing the truth that sets them free!

Justice and the poor

One of our great desires has been to include the theme of justice in our worship, not only in our singing but also in the way we live as worshippers. Several years ago we felt the Lord challenge us to give away all of our worship music instead of selling it, and to let people donate to us rather than pay a set fee for a CD. We knew that the Lord was calling us into the ministry, and as we walked on Lindisfarne (or Holy Island, off Northumbria) one afternoon, there was a very real sense that Jesus was asking us to express His outrageously generous heart.

Over the next few years this idea of making worship free continued to resonate in our hearts, and we began to pray that God would provide all the finances to enable us to record and distribute our music without selling the CDs. As we prepared to record our first live CD, *Emmanuel*, in 2004, we were challenged as to how we could use the CD to help the poor. We were encouraged by Scriptures such as Psalm 68, that place praise and justice side by side. The Psalm begins with a great swell of praise and declaration, 'Let God arise, let His enemies be scattered . . .' and continues in this theme for four verses, then changes as the psalmist reveals God's response to the injustices He sees on the earth. The Psalm continues: 'A Father of the fatherless and a judge for the widows, is God in His holy habitation. God makes a home for the lonely; He leads out the prisoners into prosperity . . . You provided in Your goodness for the poor, O God' (Psalm 68 vs 5–10).

Like this Psalm, we wanted to place our praise of the Lord and support of those in need side by side, and so we decided that, instead of paying for the CD, we would give it away and ask people instead to donate any money to a wonderful charity we partnered with called For Life, Thailand. For Life work in Thailand to rescue and transform the lives of disabled, abandoned children and they do a significant and beautiful work, which we have been able to see for ourselves. We were so encouraged and humbled by the response of people around the world who gave to their work. It became really fun to wait and see what the Lord would do next as some people took the CDs for free without donating. Some gave £1, which for many represented a significant amount of money; others gave much larger sums. We're telling our story to encourage you that the heart of God beats for the poor, and that we have a wonderful opportunity as worshippers to express that in our songwriting and our actions. The Lord loves justice (Psalm 37 v. 28), and tells us in Micah 6 v. 8 to 'do justice, to love kindness, and to walk humbly with your God'. This is how we are called to live our lives.

Something we notice as we lead worship is that if we look into the face of Jesus for long enough, enjoying His smile over our lives, we soon become aware of His tears for the broken and the poor. Let us guard ourselves from ever thinking that worship is about us and for us. It is all about Jesus, and those who worship Him will become like Him, and will find themselves acting like Him towards others. Israel fell because they 'worshipped worthless idols, only to become worthless themselves' (Jeremiah 2 v. 5, NLT). We take on the character and personality of the one our heart is surrendered to. Jesus said that where our treasure is, there our heart will be also. With our lives open to Him, we should develop a passion for the poor and lonely, as He is passionate for the poor and lonely, and seek to express that in a practical way.

One of the signs of a church that really knows how to worship is that they know how to give of their lives, resources and time to express the gratitude they feel to Jesus for His sacrifice. When our worship ends with our singing, it remains only singing, but when it flows into our actions, we begin to grasp what Jesus meant by worshipping in Spirit and in truth. When we returned from our first trip to Thailand, we were completely overwhelmed by the desperate conditions of the children in the government orphanages. We felt that one of the ways we could help motivate the church into action was to sing about the heart of God for the poor. As a result of that trip, we wrote the following song that, for us, has become an anthem to help us keep living a life of worship, and not just sing about it.

Lord, there's none like You
No one can take Your place
The Name above all names
Lord, who can compare
To Your majesty
Let all creation see

King of heaven, Lord of nations
We will bow in adoration
Glory, glory to the coming King
Join with angels singing 'holy'
Through the earth we'll give You glory
Worthy, worthy is the Lamb of God

Lord, I'll follow You
My life is in Your hands
Come, shape me for Your plans (x2)

To save the lost and feed the hungry
Clothe the naked, hold the lonely
This will be the message that we live (x2)

Hallelujah (x3)

✋ *Practical tips for worship leaders* Try to choose songs with lyrics that contain the theme of justice. It may not be in every line of the song, but look out for key phrases such as 'Defender of the weak'. By having a choice of these songs at your disposal, you'll be able to respond to the Holy Spirit when He prompts you to lead the church in this way. The important thing here is to keep people's eyes on Jesus, and not on our own agenda. We find that the best songs for this are ones that speak of His heart for justice and also praise Him within the same song. This encourages the church to live the message, but keeps Jesus at the centre. One of the dangers can be to become so focused on justice that we lose sight of the very One who brings justice into the world, but if we continue to lift up Jesus, our hearts will remain in Him.

Prophetic

Worship releases the prophetic. When earth connects with heaven it is as if the spiritual 'air' is cleared and space is created for us to hear the voice of the Lord. Psalm 95 shows us how praise and worship lead into the prophetic, as the writer begins with seven verses of worship and declaration and then says, 'Today, if you would hear His voice . . .' continuing in this prophetic vein until the end of the Psalm. The psalmist must have found himself caught up in a vision of the Lord as he praised and, within this atmosphere of worship, was then able to release the prophetic word as God spoke to him.

We also see the link between worship and the prophetic when Elisha prophesies in 2 Kings 3. He is asked by the kings of Israel, Judah and Edom to seek the Lord on their behalf, and so he asks them to bring him a minstrel, or harpist. 'And it came about, when the minstrel played, that the hand of the Lord came upon him. He said, "Thus says the Lord . . ."' (vs 15–16). Out of the place of worship Elisha prophesies the Lord's deliverance and victory to the kings.

The word of the Lord can be released in a variety of ways during a worship session, either through the worship leader in song or spoken word, or through a member of the congregation who is listening to God while worshipping. When we are leading worship we will often receive a word, Scripture, picture or impression as we're singing, and will ask the Lord who the word is for and how best to give it out. A powerful way of releasing such prophetic words is through song. This is partly because you don't tend to add in phrases such as 'I think the Lord might be saying that . . .' or, 'I'm not sure who this is for, but . . .' when you sing! You simply release what the Lord has shown you. Often we won't know the exact words to sing until they are on our lips, but we simply have a strong sense of what the Lord is wanting to say. Singing prophetically often takes a meeting to another level of anointing as people respond to the Lord and allow Him to work in their hearts.

On other occasions we use musicians to play prophetically and allow the Holy Spirit to speak to the congregation through the sound. One evening we were leading worship at Revive (the Ichthus Christian Fellowship Bible week), and felt it appropriate to ask our trumpet player to play over the congregation. He walked around the large marquee, playing his trumpet and ministering down the aisles. At times, he played triumphantly and then, at others, very quietly as he sought to respond to the Lord in his playing. From the front, we could see that people were being touched by God, each according to what the Holy Spirit was doing in their lives. After ten minutes, he returned to the stage and we continued to worship.

Unknown to any of us, a lady who worked in one of the kiosks outside the tent heard the sound of the trumpet and came in to see what was happening. She didn't know Jesus, but was touched by the presence of God as she listened to the music. Later that evening, as she spoke to the trumpeter, she gave her life to the Lord, as did the other four workers in the kiosk that week! We never know what God will do with our playing if we surrender it to Him.

Our responsibility is to stay focused on Jesus, and let Him be seen and heard. One of the great temptations in prophetic playing is to play 'in the flesh'. This is where our eyes are on ourselves, and we simply perform a solo to impress others, but this makes us nothing more than a 'noisy gong' or 'clanging cymbal' (1 Corinthians 13 v. 1) no matter how 'good' we sound. To be prophetic, we need to learn how to lean on the Lord and listen to Him as we play, so that we might release His presence.

Practical tips for worship leaders Encourage the congregation to sing in tongues. Paul tells us in 1 Corinthians 14 v. 4 that the gift of tongues edifies the individual. It helps us to connect with the presence of the Lord as we leave space for Him to fill our hearts and minds with His words, rather than our own. For those who don't speak in tongues, encourage them to sing spontaneous praise in their own language. As people begin to sing from their hearts, it will focus their minds and connect them with the Lord, giving Him a channel through which to speak.

If you want to learn to prophesy in song or on your instrument, you need to practise hearing His voice and singing or playing prophetically in the hidden place. Then you can have confidence in the public arena, not in your own ability but rather in hearing His voice, or prompting, and knowing how to respond to it. As you become accustomed to His still, small voice in your everyday life, you'll be able to discern it when leading worship or playing. To get you started, try worshipping out of Scripture. Take a passage, such as a Psalm, and begin to sing the words or play your instrument as you read. As you do this, the living word of God will begin to live in you and you will find yourself repeating or elaborating on phrases, responding to the Holy Spirit as He leads you. Familiarising yourself with verses from Scripture is very useful, as the Lord can then call them to mind when you are leading worship so that you can sing their truth over the congregation.

It takes some courage to develop this gifting as it can feel quite exposing, but the more you step out in boldness, the more you'll know God is there to meet you and use you to release His word in power. Be careful not to embellish the word God has given with your own 'thoughts', as it dilutes the power of the word. Simply give out what you have been given by Him, and trust God to do the rest. It's often the short prophetic songs or words that are the most effective in communicating the heart of God.

Lament
One of the most challenging dynamics during a worship

time is the lament. It is an area of worship that isn't widely explored, as it is difficult to maintain a balance between mourning over the sin of a nation or the state of hearts and lives and, at the same time, expressing the hope that comes from Jesus. We don't want to depress our congregations with songs that simply mourn, as we have a Saviour who tells us to take heart because He has overcome the world!

If you read through the Psalms, you will find many occasions when the psalmist laments and asks 'how long' things will remain as they are. However, in these same passages there are also declarations of the character of God, and statements of faith about how He will intervene. Psalm 94 says, 'How long shall the wicked, O Lord, how long shall the wicked exult? . . . They band themselves together against the life of the righteous and condemn the innocent to death. But the Lord has been my stronghold, and my God the rock of my refuge . . . The Lord our God will destroy them' (vs 3, 21–23). It is not wrong to express our hearts before the Lord! He desires us to be real with Him, but He also wants us to remember who He is and what He will do when His people seek Him. Let us remind our congregations that He is the God of hope, who can do more than we can ask or imagine.

✋ ***Practical tips for worship leaders*** Make sure that your songs of lament also contain the hope of the gospel.

We would often use a song of this style in the context of a prayer meeting, where people can use the words to intercede, rather than on a Sunday morning when we are trying to cater for all ages and all levels of spiritual maturity. If the lament does not lead us to pray, it will simply stir our emotions, but will have no effect in changing things on earth.

7 Covered by His Presence

As worship leaders, we are constantly seeking to open up a way for people to encounter the presence of God. Our desire is to help our congregations fix their eyes on Jesus and 'keep seeking the things above, where Christ is, seated at the right hand of God' (Colossians 3 v. 1). With this as our goal, it is not surprising that the role of worship leader is a contested one, in which we will encounter spiritual pressure. However, in this same 'dwelling place' where we experience intimacy with Him, we can also receive His covering, as Psalm 91 reminds us. 'He will cover you with His pinions, and under His wings you may seek refuge' (Psalm 91 v. 4). We need to remember to ask for the covering of His presence, and have faith that He will answer us.

The Scriptures are full of accounts and images that speak of the covering of our God. In Exodus 12 we read of the Passover, in which the Lord saves His people from destruction and makes a way for them to be released from their oppressor. As with many Old Testament accounts, these events foreshadow what Jesus will come and achieve for us in the flesh in the New Testament, and we can look to them and place our hope in the same God who works on our behalf. Our faith and confidence can be drawn from this: that if the blood of a lamb, applied in obedience to the Lord, can hold back the destroyer, how much more will the blood of Jesus, taken hold of again in obedience to the Lord, hold back the destroyer from our own lives.

We can draw three parallels from this Passover account that will empower us as we seek to be covered by His presence. The first is very simply that they knew they had an enemy, and they knew who that enemy was. If you are not aware that you have an enemy who is seeking to stop you from breaking into the presence of the Lord, you won't be prepared to stand and defend yourself. You will be like one who stumbles onto a battlefield anticipating a country walk, but encounters a hail of arrows instead! We need to be aware that we have an enemy who does not want us to live in intimacy with the Lord, as he knows the incredible power that comes as a result.

We also need to be aware *who* our enemy is. All too often we look to earthly, natural things, when our mind should be grasping the spiritual and supernatural things. We assume our enemy is the member of our band who is always difficult towards us, or the PA operator, or the equipment itself, or a whole host of other people or things that seem to assail us when we come to lead worship. We need to ask for discernment as we prepare in prayer, so that we are aware of the enemy's specific tactics against us, even if they come through one or all of the above! When we are seeing through heaven's eyes, we will be able to address situations spiritually and deal with relationships and equipment as Jesus would.

The second lesson we can draw from the Passover account is to *apply* the blood of Jesus as the Israelites applied the blood of their lambs. This application was imperative. They could have slain their lambs in accordance with the command of the Lord, but if they had left the blood in the basin in their homes, they would have fallen under the same destruction as the Egyptians. Without the application of the blood, they too would have lost the firstborn of every family. The Lord instructs them to apply the blood of the lamb, and says that when He sees the blood on the lintel and on the two doorposts, He will pass over the door and will not allow the destroyer to come into their houses to smite them (Exodus 12 v. 23).

In the same way that the Israelites were not saved simply because they were His people, we are not protected simply because we are Christians. We are called to exercise our faith and take hold of His truths, applying the blood of Jesus through believing prayer and declaration. As we do so, we stand in Jesus' authority, reminding ourselves, and the heavenly realms, of Christ's victory and of our own status in Him. He is the triumphant King! We are sons and daughters of the King and, as such, we can claim a royal guard. This also reminds Satan that he is a defeated foe, as the blood speaks of Christ's ultimate victory over the evil one. As we pray, we are asking that we might see the reality of that ultimate victory here on earth in our own situations. We declare to ourselves and to the spiritual realm that victory, authority and power belong to the Lord, and we ask that everything in our lives comes into line with that reality. As we grasp hold of this truth and let its power work in our lives, we will see the devil flee!

The third parallel for us from this Passover account concerns boundaries. Not only did the Israelites need to apply the blood, but they were also given one further instruction: '. . . none of you shall go outside the door of his house until morning' (Exodus 12 v. 22). Again, they could have followed the command of the Lord and killed the Passover lamb; they could even have applied the blood to the lintel and two doorposts, but if they had not stayed within the boundaries that the Lord had set, they would have incurred the same devastation as the Egyptians. Obedience was key.

This is exactly the same for us as we seek the covering of the Lord. Ephesians 4 v. 27 warns us: 'Do not give the devil an opportunity' (literally 'a place'). When thinking about our own spiritual protection, we mustn't give the devil a 'landing pad' in our lives, either through what we say or think or do, as this gives him an authority we really don't want him to have. Rather, we need to be asking the Lord to search our hearts and see if there is any offensive way in us (Psalm 139 vs 23–24), so that we can, if necessary, repent and walk back inside His boundaries.

On occasion, before a meeting, we sometimes feel the Lord prompting us to stay away from conversations with people. We can remember one particular time when we didn't heed the warning of the Lord and, in essence, were disobedient. We ended up engaging in a very unhelpful conversation, which meant that our minds were distracted as we came to lead worship. We had walked outside of the Lord's boundary. He sets these boundaries for our good, and if we stay within them, we will know that sense of living under the shelter of His wings.

8 Leading Worship: Practical Steps

There are many practical aspects to leading worship which work alongside the spiritual. Our ability to execute simple, practical steps during a worship session will often determine whether or not a congregation is able to press into the presence of God. If we get the practical side right, no one will even notice we are there – which is how it should be – but if we don't, the church will be all too aware of our presence!

The following practical steps are by no means an exhaustive list, or the only way of doing things, but rather things that we have found to be helpful as we have sought to lead others in worship.

Prepare through prayer
The first thing to do when preparing for a worship time is to ask the Lord what He is saying about the meeting. Everything should flow from listening to His voice. Pray for your band members. Pray about which songs to choose. Pray for a smooth time with the technical equipment. Pray that the congregation would see and hear Jesus as they worship. Pray for your own heart

and mind to be able to perceive clearly what the Holy Spirit is saying, and will go on to say during the session. Colossians 4 v. 2 tells us to devote ourselves to prayer, keeping alert in it with an attitude of thanksgiving, and 1 Peter 5 v. 8 tells us to be on the alert since our adversary, the devil, prowls around like a roaring lion, seeking someone to devour. Watchfulness in prayer will alert us to the devil's schemes, and will give us an opportunity to address these spiritually before we arrive to lead worship.

Prayer will prepare our hearts so that we can hear the 'now' word of God, and not rest on past revelation. This doesn't prevent us from accessing material from the past, but it will be because of revelation rather than habit. A song that feels anointed one week may not have the same effect the week after, as the Lord may be emphasising something different. The challenge for the worship leader is to know what God is saying, and to select songs that will serve as a vehicle through which this can be heard.

Choosing the right songs . . . and beyond!
Think about the size, age and maturity of the congregation, and try to have realistic expectations about your song choices. For example, it would be no good choosing all the latest youth-based material for

a congregation of elderly people, and expect them to engage. We need to use songs that are suitable for the occasion or congregation, asking ourselves whether we need celebration songs, intimate songs, family worship songs, warfare songs, and so on. If you are preparing for a Sunday morning or a celebration, it can be good to begin with upbeat, declaratory songs which speak of the power and majesty of God. These help to lift people's eyes off what they have just come from and place them on the Lord. Remember that worship is like going on a journey, and these songs will often serve as an entry point. Once we have 'entered in', we can then begin to minister more specifically what the Lord has been revealing to us.

When building a worship set, we often feel the Lord highlighting a particular song that goes along with the word He has given us for the meeting. We rarely use this song at the beginning of the worship set, as it can take two or three songs to engage a congregation, and we don't want to lose the impact of this moment while we are still gathering people together. In other words, we seek to spend time drawing people into the prophetic words the Lord has given us.

We all have our favourite songs, and it can be tempting to sing the material we enjoy most, but since the congregation will vary in musical taste, it is worth mixing up the material to include a variety of songs that will engage people right across the church. Remember that we are there to serve others, not ourselves. Try not to get stuck in always doing the same songs. It can be too easy to rely on old set lists that, in time, begin to look a bit tired and predictable. With time spent learning new songs and rediscovering old ones, we will hopefully achieve both depth and freshness.

By understanding our congregation, we should be able to meet them where they are and take them on a journey into the Lord's presence. Once they have begun to engage with the Lord, we can then break new spiritual ground and try out new songs, shouts, dancing, prayer, prophetic worship and singing in tongues. If the church is experienced in worshipping and comfortable with pressing into the presence of the Lord, we are presented with a wonderful opportunity to 'enter in' and spend a significant amount of time in His presence. When this happens, we love to lead people in what we call going 'off the map'. This is where we use a few songs to gather people together to build spiritual agreements, and then use the faith that has risen and been released in that time to leave the route of singing set songs, and begin to sing in tongues and rely on the Holy Spirit to direct our path. From this will flow prophetic songs in our own language, perhaps from Scripture or visions we have seen, and songs in His heavenly language. If the congregation is fully engaged in this, and a new sense of life is rising, it can be effective to sing short, simple phrases such as 'Jesus is Lord' as a launch pad to take people deeper. We have found this to be a very powerful way of leading worship, and have seen it change the direction of entire worship sessions as the Holy Spirit takes control of the meeting.

If you sense that your congregation is not yet ready to step out in this way, don't force it as it will only serve to bring disagreements. Instead, through prayer and gradually introducing these practices in small measures, people will hopefully learn to linger in the Lord's presence and be led by the Holy Spirit. One very helpful way of making the congregation feel confident is for us to lead confidently from the front! Ensure your instructions are audible. Often we drop our voices when we speak into the microphone rather than sing, and people may not have heard you when you invited them to sing their own songs to the Lord. Also, if you step away from the microphone and can't be heard as you sing out, the likelihood will be that the congregation too won't sing very loudly. They will always sing more quietly than you!

Are the songs in the best musical keys?
One of the difficulties we have in our congregational

worship is that men and women have different vocal ranges, and therefore it can be hard to pitch a song in a key that suits everyone. We will never be able to cater for all voices at all times, but it is helpful to think these things through when choosing our songs. One factor to consider is the number of people we have in our worship gathering. For example, if we are leading worship in a housegroup setting, it is better to sing in a lower key as people only tend to be happy to sing high notes if they are not going to be heard! In a congregation or celebration setting, this doesn't tend to be such an issue as people will sing more loudly, which actually helps them to reach the higher notes. A good rule of thumb for a larger meeting is to keep the high notes no higher than a top D on the scale.

Do the songs flow?

In certain contexts it can be helpful for the songs to flow together in the same musical key in order that we can keep everyone's eyes on Jesus and not on the band. Long intros and outros can be fantastic in the right context, such as a larger celebration, but sometimes they can be a distraction and draw people's attention away from the Lord. There is a time and place for more elaborate music in our worship sessions, as it can help to release praise, but it must always serve to fix the congregation's eyes on

Jesus and not distract them from Him.

We often find it helpful to put three or four songs together in the same musical key so that we can flow seamlessly between them. (This works for both 'fast' and 'slow' songs, provided the faster songs are played at a similar tempo, otherwise it will feel more like a collision than a flow!) When we're singing slower, more intimate songs, linking them together can be particularly powerful as it provides the opportunity to keep pressing into the Lord and soaking up His presence without interruption. When you gather together as a band to rehearse or, even better, to worship together, practise linking songs so that all your musicians can do this with ease. The more you work with the same musicians, the more aware they will become of your next move.

Do we have the gifting in the band to carry the songs musically?

Practise your instrument regularly. David was a skilled musician and required the same of others (1 Chronicles 25 v. 7). Of course, the Lord does not require a certain standard of musicianship before we can participate in worship, but we do want to keep offering Him our best. It will also give us more confidence as we stand in front of others if we know we have already mastered a song for ourselves! The more proficient we become at our instruments, the more confident we'll feel to lead people in worship, and the congregation will feel confident to worship with us.

We need to be released from feeling pressured to use 'big' songs if we've got a small and inexperienced band. It is far better to use songs that the band is comfortable with than attempt to reach musical heights that will expose limitations. As the band rehearses together, these more complex songs or arrangements may become more attainable.

Do we know the music and words well enough?

It can be quite distracting for a congregation when a worship leader has to sort through his or her music in between songs as it can, again, break the flow of the worship session. If we're not able to learn the songs by heart – which is the ideal – then the music should be there preferably to serve as a reminder rather than relied on to make it through the song.

Leading worship is the ultimate act of multitasking as it involves singing, playing an instrument (for many worship leaders), listening to and leading the band, watching the congregation to make sure they're following you, listening to the Lord for His leading and keeping an eye on the meeting leader for any instruction that he or she may wish to give to you. If you have to add to this the task of reading music/chords as well, it is quite possible that one of the other areas will suffer.

We are aware that not everyone is able to learn the songs by heart, and we certainly wouldn't prevent a worship leader from serving simply because they couldn't remember the songs, but it is something worth aiming for. Try to begin the process of committing at least one song to memory each time you lead worship or play. You will then soon build up your own treasury of songs that you can play 'by ear'.

Another benefit of learning the music by heart is that we can respond to the Holy Spirit and the congregation with any change of direction without having to find the song in our folders. Many times we have found that we've had to change the song list during a session because people are not engaging, and knowing the songs by heart has enabled us to flow wherever we've needed to.

Does the congregation know the song?

A helpful pattern for introducing a new song is the **3-1-1** rule. This is where we introduce a new song and use it for three weeks in a row, and then give it a week's rest before using it again. If it works well after the week's rest, then you'll know your congregation has grasped it.

As a general rule, we try not to introduce more than

one new song in a worship session. If people have to keep learning new songs during the same set, it can prevent them from really relaxing into the time of worship. Obviously there are exceptions to the rule, but we've found this to be a good starting point.

Are the song words appearing correctly on the screen?
It can be a hindrance to the congregation if the words being projected onto the screen are different to the words being sung by the worship leader, or are simply badly spelled. It is a good idea to check before the meeting to make sure the songs are all written correctly on the computer or acetate.

Leading worship without an instrument
If you are leading worship without an instrument, it is essential to choose one musician in your band who you can work with closely and who can communicate with the other musicians for you, much like the musical director described in the chapter on team dynamics. This will usually be a pianist/keyboard player or an acoustic guitarist, and they will provide your greatest support. They will need to be totally familiar with all your material and be a competent player, so that you can have the confidence to know that they will always be able to follow you.

Communication during the worship session is obviously more of a challenge without an instrument. A worship leader who leads with a guitar or piano/keyboard can decrease in volume, which lets the band and congregation know that he or she is intending to move into a quieter moment, or they can end a song by playing the last line more slowly, and then begin another song. Without an instrument, you are going to need to develop other ways of communicating. One way is to use your voice to sing or speak instructions to the band and congregation. For example, you can sing/speak the first few words of the verse or chorus you want to go into, or say simple instructions like 'last time' or 'verse two'.

Another very useful way of communicating is to use hand signals. You will need to develop these with your own musicians, but ones we have developed are signals for repeating a verse or chorus, decreasing the volume and ending a song. The more you use these with your musicians, the more they will be able to understand and follow your lead. If possible, it is helpful to have another strong vocalist with you as this gives you the ability to step back for a moment, knowing the vocal line is still being held, and communicate with your band if all other attempts have failed!

Linking songs together in the same key is more

essential if you lead without an instrument. Having at least three or four songs together will give you the freedom to move easily between songs without needing to stop and wait for your lead musician to start up again. It will leave you feeling more in control – that you are the one who is doing the leading.

The use of musical space and silence

Some of the most precious moments in our 'sung' worship times can be when there is actually no singing at all. Psalm 46 v. 10 tells us to 'be still' (or *silent*), and know that He is God (NLT). If you're anything like us, moments of silence are rare in everyday life. Our ears always seem to be full of something – phone calls, music, television, family, friends, colleagues. Creating moments of silence within our worship sessions will give people a rare opportunity to get away from the 'noise' of everyday life and hear the voice of the Lord. In these 'waiting' or 'listening' times we are able to draw from the life and energy of His presence. Isaiah 40 v. 31 reminds us that '. . . those who wait for the Lord will gain new strength; they will mount up with wings like eagles, they will run and not get tired, they will walk and not become weary'.

Another way of providing 'space' in a worship time in order for the congregation to listen to the Lord, or simply rest in Him, is to allow solo instruments to minister over the congregation as they focus on Jesus. We have found that this not only refreshes souls, but also opens hearts to hear His voice. Out of these moments we often find that prophetic songs begin to rise up within us, which we'll then sing over the people as the Lord leads.

In these moments of musical space and silence it can be helpful to communicate with the congregation so that they can relax and receive, otherwise you may find people watching you, wondering why 'nothing' is happening. There will, of course, be times when God is moving so powerfully in the meeting that you won't need to say anything, as everyone will be captivated by His presence, and silence will fall naturally, out of reverence and a healthy fear of the Lord.

Overall, the most important thing about the use of musical space and silence in our sung worship is timing. If silence and space are used at the wrong time, it will feel like we are losing the focus of the meeting. However, in its right place it will refresh the body of Christ and draw them deeper into His presence.

A Meditation

All too often the enemy seeks to contest our right to minister before the Lord. Hebrews 9 and 10 remind us that we minister because of Him, in Him and for Him. Let us take hold of the marvellous truths of these passages as we fix our eyes on Jesus and stand firm to serve Him with all that we are.

Hebrews 9 v. 24 *For Christ did not enter a holy place made with hands, a mere copy of the true one, but into heaven itself, now to appear in the presence of God for us;*

Christ is our advocate. Our intercessor. Ever there to represent us. Totally human. Totally divine. He who is for us and not against us. He, through whom we can have access, through whom we can draw near, appears in the presence of God for us.

Vs 25–26 *Nor was it that He would offer Himself often, as the high priest enters the holy place year by year with blood that is not his own. Otherwise, He would have needed to suffer often since the foundation of the world; but now once at the consummation of the ages He has been manifested to put away sin by the sacrifice of Himself.*

Sin is 'put away'! It is finished! We do not need to be stuck in its burdensome cycle any more. It is put away! Out of our sight, if we choose to gaze upon Jesus . . .

9 vs 27–28 *And inasmuch as it is appointed for men to die once and after this comes judgement, so Christ also, having been offered once to bear the sins of many, will appear a second time for salvation without reference to sin, to those who eagerly await Him.*

Our God is so much bigger than sin that He dealt with it all once, for all time, for all people, for every sin – every thought, every word, every deed – and He looks for those who will eagerly await Him.

10 vs 1–10 *For the Law, since it has only a shadow of the good things to come and not the very form of things, can never, by the same sacrifices which they offer continually year by year, make perfect those who draw near. Otherwise, would they not have ceased to be offered, because the worshippers, having once been cleansed, would no longer have had consciousness of sins? But in those sacrifices there is a reminder of sins year by year. For it is impossible for the blood of bulls and goats to take away sins. Therefore, when He comes into the world, He says, 'Sacrifice and offering You have not desired, but a body you have prepared for Me; in whole burnt offerings and*

sacrifices for sin You have taken no pleasure.' Then I said, 'Behold, I have come (in the scroll of the book it is written of Me) to do Your will, O God.' After saying above, 'Sacrifices and offerings and whole burnt offerings and sacrifices for sin You have not desired, nor have You taken pleasure in them' (which are offered according to the Law), then He said, 'Behold, I have come to do Your will.' He takes away the first in order to establish the second. By this will we have been sanctified through the offering of the body of Jesus Christ once for all.

It is the will of Jesus that we draw near. It is the will of Jesus that our sin is dealt with so that we can enjoy fellowship with Him, close fellowship again. His will was stated in Garden of Gethsemane, 'Not mine, but Yours, Father.' That was His will. Because He did it, He has made it possible for us also to do it . . . for us to bend our fleshly wills to the will of the Father. He 'wills' us to be in relationship with Him. We can also 'will' to be free from our sin and fleshliness and choose to be in relationship with Him, because He has made a way.

10 vs 11–14 *Every priest stands daily ministering and offering time after time the same sacrifices, which can never take away sins; but He, having offered one sacrifice for sins for all time, sat down at the right hand of God, waiting from*

that time onward until His enemies be made a footstool for His feet. For by one offering He has perfected for all time those who are sanctified.

One sacrifice for sins for all time. Let us not belittle the work of Jesus on the cross by thinking that it is not powerful enough to deal with our sin. He did it. He offered Himself, and then He sat down, and you don't sit down until the job is done! The job *is* done. It is finished. Our sin has been dealt with. The gap has been bridged, and now we can draw near . . . nearer . . . nearer still to the presence of our God.

10 vs 15–17 *And the Holy Spirit also testifies to us; for after saying, 'This is the covenant that I will make with them after those days, says the Lord: I will put My laws upon their heart, and on their mind I will write them,' He then says, 'And their sins and their lawless deeds I will remember no more.'*

Our sins, our faults, our shortcomings, they are not remembered! When we give them to Jesus, they are no longer taken account of. They have gone . . . so let it go. He keeps no record of wrongs. That's true love, and He is love.

10 v. 18 *Now where there is forgiveness of these things, there*

is no longer any offering for sin.

This is our evidence that we have forgiveness when we come to Jesus . . . because there is no longer any offering for sins. This is our evidence that our sin is dealt with. Let us step into that reality. Let us draw near with confidence!

10 vs 19–22 Therefore, brethren, since we have confidence to enter the holy place by the blood of Jesus, by a new and living way which He inaugurated for us through the veil, that is, His flesh, and since we have a great priest over the house of God, let us draw near

We are given the way in (through His flesh) and the way in is still open. The Great Priest is ever there to welcome us . . . so we can draw near . . .

with a sincere heart

Once we have come to Jesus and have been remade, we can hold our lives up to the light and know that we are sincere . . . not because of our own merit, but because of His grace. We are saved by His faithfulness, not our own faith.

in full assurance of faith, having our hearts sprinkled clean from an evil conscience and our bodies washed with pure water.

We still need washing and sprinkling. Jesus said to Peter, 'He who has bathed needs only to wash His feet, but is completely clean; and you are clean' (John 13 v. 10). Let us be those who keep clean . . . who keep coming to Jesus to have our sins dealt with, so we can keep drawing near.

10 vs 23–25 *Let us hold fast the confession of our hope without wavering, for He who promised is faithful; and let us consider how to stimulate one another to love and good deeds, not forsaking our own assembling together, as is the habit of some, but encouraging one another; and all the more as you see the day drawing near.*

Keep drawing near, for the day is drawing near . . .

The triumph of the cross
Death has lost its sting
Swallowed up in victory
That we might live in Him
Seated now with Christ
At the Father's side
Out of darkness, one with Him
Raised to glorious life

Copyright details